50 Premium Thailand Dishes

By: Kelly Johnson

Table of Contents

- Tom Yum Goong (Spicy Shrimp Soup)
- Massaman Curry
- Pad Thai
- Green Curry (Gaeng Keow Wan)
- Panang Curry
- Som Tum (Green Papaya Salad)
- Tom Kha Gai (Coconut Chicken Soup)
- Gaeng Daeng (Red Curry)
- Moo Pad Krapow (Basil Pork Stir-Fry)
- Pla Pao (Grilled Fish)
- Pad See Ew (Stir-Fried Noodles with Soy Sauce)
- Khao Soi (Northern Thai Curry Noodles)
- Gai Yang (Grilled Chicken)
- Larb (Spicy Minced Meat Salad)
- Massaman Gai (Chicken Massaman Curry)
- Khao Pad (Thai Fried Rice)
- Goong Pad Saparot (Pineapple Fried Rice with Shrimp)
- Nam Tok Moo (Grilled Pork Salad)
- Khao Niew Mamuang (Mango Sticky Rice)
- Tom Yum Goong Nam Khon (Creamy Spicy Shrimp Soup)
- Hor Mok (Steamed Fish Curry)
- Moo Satay (Grilled Pork Skewers)
- Kanom Jeen (Rice Noodles with Curry)
- Baked Mussels with Glass Noodles
- Gaeng Kari (Yellow Curry)
- Pad Krapow Gai (Basil Chicken Stir-Fry)
- Kaeng Phet (Spicy Red Curry)
- Khai Jiao (Thai Omelette)
- Tod Man Pla (Thai Fish Cakes)
- Yum Nua (Spicy Beef Salad)
- Tom Zap (Sour and Spicy Soup)
- Khao Mun Gai (Chicken Rice)
- Kuay Tiew (Thai Noodle Soup)
- Pla Rad Prik (Fried Fish with Chili Sauce)
- Moo Hong (Braised Pork Belly)

- Gaeng Pa (Jungle Curry)
- Kanom Krok (Coconut Rice Pancakes)
- Yod Woon Sen (Glass Noodle Salad)
- Moo Pad King (Stir-Fried Pork with Ginger)
- Moo Nam Tok (Waterfall Pork Salad)
- Goong Mung Krob (Crispy Shrimp)
- Khao Pad Kung (Shrimp Fried Rice)
- Pad Kee Mao (Drunken Noodles)
- Som Tum Thai (Spicy Thai Papaya Salad)
- Gai Pad Med Mamuang (Chicken with Cashew Nuts)
- Nam Prik Ong (Spicy Tomato Dip)
- Pad Pak Bung Fai Daeng (Stir-Fried Morning Glory)
- Pla Nueng Manao (Steamed Fish with Lime)
- Khao Chae (Rice in Jasmine Scented Water)
- Nua Pad Prik (Beef with Chili Sauce)

Tom Yum Goong (Spicy Shrimp Soup)

Ingredients:

- 1 lb shrimp, peeled and deveined
- 4 cups water or chicken broth
- 3 stalks lemongrass, smashed
- 3 kaffir lime leaves, torn
- 3-4 Thai bird's eye chilies, smashed
- 1-inch piece galangal, sliced
- 200g mushrooms, sliced
- 2 medium tomatoes, quartered
- 2 tablespoons fish sauce
- 1 tablespoon sugar
- 1 tablespoon lime juice
- Fresh cilantro leaves for garnish

Instructions:

1. Bring water or broth to a boil in a pot. Add lemongrass, kaffir lime leaves, chilies, and galangal. Simmer for 5 minutes.
2. Add mushrooms and tomatoes. Simmer until softened.
3. Add shrimp, fish sauce, sugar, and lime juice. Cook until shrimp are pink.
4. Adjust seasoning if needed, then remove from heat.
5. Garnish with fresh cilantro and serve hot.

Massaman Curry

Ingredients:

- 1 lb beef or chicken, cubed
- 1 can coconut milk
- 2 tablespoons Massaman curry paste
- 1 onion, chopped
- 2 potatoes, cubed
- 1/2 cup roasted peanuts
- 1 tablespoon fish sauce
- 1 tablespoon sugar
- 2 cinnamon sticks
- 2 cardamom pods
- Salt to taste

Instructions:

1. Heat a pot and add curry paste, cooking for 2-3 minutes.
2. Add meat and sear on all sides. Add onions and cook until soft.
3. Pour in coconut milk, potatoes, peanuts, cinnamon, and cardamom.
4. Simmer for 30-40 minutes until meat and potatoes are tender.
5. Season with fish sauce, sugar, and salt. Serve with rice.

Pad Thai

Ingredients:

- 8 oz rice noodles
- 1/2 lb shrimp or chicken, sliced
- 2 eggs, beaten
- 1/4 cup tamarind paste
- 3 tablespoons fish sauce
- 2 tablespoons sugar
- 1 tablespoon lime juice
- 2 cloves garlic, minced
- 2 tablespoons vegetable oil
- 1/4 cup roasted peanuts, chopped
- Fresh cilantro and lime wedges for garnish

Instructions:

1. Cook rice noodles according to package instructions.
2. Heat oil in a pan and cook garlic, then add shrimp or chicken. Cook until pink.
3. Push protein to the side and scramble eggs in the same pan.
4. Add noodles, tamarind paste, fish sauce, sugar, and lime juice. Toss to coat.
5. Garnish with peanuts, cilantro, and lime wedges. Serve hot.

Green Curry (Gaeng Keow Wan)

Ingredients:

- 1 lb chicken or beef, sliced
- 2 tablespoons green curry paste
- 1 can coconut milk
- 1/2 cup chicken broth
- 1 eggplant, sliced
- 1 red bell pepper, sliced
- 1/2 cup Thai basil leaves
- 2 tablespoons fish sauce
- 1 tablespoon sugar
- Kaffir lime leaves (optional)

Instructions:

1. Heat a pot and add green curry paste. Stir-fry for 2-3 minutes.
2. Add coconut milk, chicken broth, chicken, eggplant, and bell pepper. Simmer for 15-20 minutes.
3. Season with fish sauce, sugar, and optional lime leaves.
4. Garnish with Thai basil and serve with rice.

Panang Curry

Ingredients:

- 1 lb beef or chicken, sliced
- 2 tablespoons Panang curry paste
- 1 can coconut milk
- 1/4 cup chicken broth
- 2 tablespoons fish sauce
- 1 tablespoon sugar
- 1 tablespoon lime juice
- Kaffir lime leaves (optional)
- Fresh basil leaves for garnish

Instructions:

1. Heat a pot and add curry paste. Stir-fry for 2 minutes.
2. Add coconut milk and chicken broth, bring to a simmer.
3. Add meat, fish sauce, sugar, and lime juice. Simmer for 15 minutes.
4. Garnish with basil leaves and serve with rice.

Som Tum (Green Papaya Salad)

Ingredients:

- 2 cups shredded green papaya
- 1 carrot, shredded
- 1/4 cup peanuts, crushed
- 2-3 Thai bird's eye chilies, smashed
- 2 cloves garlic, smashed
- 2 tablespoons fish sauce
- 1 tablespoon sugar
- 2 tablespoons lime juice
- 1 tablespoon palm sugar (optional)
- 1 tomato, quartered

Instructions:

1. In a mortar, pound garlic and chilies until mashed.
2. Add peanuts, fish sauce, sugar, lime juice, and palm sugar, and mix well.
3. Add shredded papaya, carrot, and tomatoes. Toss everything together.
4. Serve immediately with sticky rice.

Tom Kha Gai (Coconut Chicken Soup)

Ingredients:

- 1 lb chicken breast, sliced
- 4 cups coconut milk
- 3 stalks lemongrass, smashed
- 3 kaffir lime leaves, torn
- 1-inch piece galangal, sliced
- 3 Thai bird's eye chilies, smashed
- 200g mushrooms, sliced
- 2 tablespoons fish sauce
- 2 tablespoons lime juice
- Fresh cilantro for garnish

Instructions:

1. In a pot, bring coconut milk to a simmer. Add lemongrass, kaffir lime leaves, galangal, and chilies.
2. Add chicken and mushrooms, simmer for 10 minutes.
3. Stir in fish sauce and lime juice.
4. Remove from heat and garnish with cilantro. Serve hot.

Gaeng Daeng (Red Curry)

Ingredients:

- 1 lb chicken or beef, sliced
- 2 tablespoons red curry paste
- 1 can coconut milk
- 1/2 cup chicken broth
- 1/2 cup bamboo shoots, sliced
- 1 red bell pepper, sliced
- 1 tablespoon fish sauce
- 1 tablespoon sugar
- Fresh basil leaves for garnish

Instructions:

1. Heat a pot and stir-fry red curry paste for 2 minutes.
2. Add coconut milk, chicken broth, meat, bamboo shoots, and bell pepper. Simmer for 15 minutes.
3. Season with fish sauce, sugar, and adjust to taste.
4. Garnish with basil leaves and serve with rice.

Moo Pad Krapow (Basil Pork Stir-Fry)

Ingredients:

- 1 lb ground pork
- 2 cloves garlic, minced
- 2-3 Thai bird's eye chilies, chopped
- 1 tablespoon fish sauce
- 1 tablespoon soy sauce
- 1 teaspoon sugar
- 1/2 cup Thai basil leaves
- 2 tablespoons vegetable oil

Instructions:

1. Heat oil in a pan and sauté garlic and chilies until fragrant.
2. Add ground pork and cook until browned.
3. Stir in fish sauce, soy sauce, and sugar. Cook for 2 minutes.
4. Add basil leaves and cook until wilted. Serve hot with rice.

Pla Pao (Grilled Fish)

Ingredients:

- 1 whole fish (tilapia or snapper)
- 2 stalks lemongrass, smashed
- 3 kaffir lime leaves, torn
- 2-3 Thai bird's eye chilies
- 3 cloves garlic, minced
- 1 tablespoon fish sauce
- 1 tablespoon soy sauce
- Salt to taste
- Lime wedges for garnish

Instructions:

1. Clean and gut the fish, then make a few slashes on each side.
2. Stuff the fish with lemongrass, lime leaves, chilies, and garlic.
3. Rub the fish with fish sauce, soy sauce, and salt.
4. Grill over medium heat for 10-15 minutes on each side, or until cooked through.
5. Serve with lime wedges.

Pad See Ew (Stir-Fried Noodles with Soy Sauce)

Ingredients:

- 8 oz wide rice noodles
- 1/2 lb chicken or beef, sliced
- 2 tablespoons soy sauce
- 1 tablespoon dark soy sauce
- 1 tablespoon oyster sauce
- 2 eggs, beaten
- 2 cups broccoli or Chinese broccoli
- 2 tablespoons vegetable oil
- 2 cloves garlic, minced

Instructions:

1. Cook noodles according to package instructions, drain, and set aside.
2. In a wok, heat oil and sauté garlic until fragrant.
3. Add meat and cook until browned. Push to the side.
4. Add eggs and scramble them, then add noodles, soy sauce, dark soy sauce, and oyster sauce.
5. Stir-fry, then add broccoli and cook until tender.
6. Serve hot.

Khao Soi (Northern Thai Curry Noodles)

Ingredients:

- 1 lb chicken or beef
- 2 tablespoons red curry paste
- 1 can coconut milk
- 3 cups chicken broth
- 2 tablespoons fish sauce
- 1 tablespoon sugar
- 1 package egg noodles
- 1/2 cup fried shallots
- Lime wedges for garnish

Instructions:

1. Cook the egg noodles according to package instructions and set aside.
2. In a pot, heat curry paste and cook for 2 minutes. Add coconut milk and chicken broth, then bring to a boil.
3. Add meat, fish sauce, and sugar. Simmer for 30 minutes.
4. Serve the soup over noodles, garnished with fried shallots and lime wedges.

Gai Yang (Grilled Chicken)

Ingredients:

- 1 whole chicken, spatchcocked (or 4 chicken breasts)
- 3 cloves garlic, minced
- 2 tablespoons soy sauce
- 2 tablespoons fish sauce
- 1 tablespoon lime juice
- 1 tablespoon palm sugar
- 1 tablespoon turmeric powder
- Fresh cilantro for garnish

Instructions:

1. Combine garlic, soy sauce, fish sauce, lime juice, palm sugar, and turmeric to make a marinade.
2. Marinate the chicken for at least 2 hours.
3. Grill the chicken over medium heat for 15-20 minutes on each side, until golden brown and cooked through.
4. Garnish with fresh cilantro and serve with rice.

Larb (Spicy Minced Meat Salad)

Ingredients:

- 1 lb ground pork or chicken
- 1 tablespoon fish sauce
- 1 tablespoon lime juice
- 1 tablespoon chili flakes
- 1 teaspoon sugar
- 1/2 cup fresh mint leaves
- 1/2 cup cilantro leaves
- 1/2 red onion, thinly sliced
- Lettuce leaves for serving

Instructions:

1. Cook the ground meat in a pan until browned.
2. In a bowl, mix fish sauce, lime juice, chili flakes, and sugar.
3. Add cooked meat to the bowl and stir to combine.
4. Add mint, cilantro, and red onion, then mix well.
5. Serve wrapped in lettuce leaves.

Massaman Gai (Chicken Massaman Curry)

Ingredients:

- 1 lb chicken, cut into pieces
- 2 tablespoons Massaman curry paste
- 1 can coconut milk
- 1/2 cup chicken broth
- 2 potatoes, cubed
- 1/4 cup roasted peanuts
- 2 cinnamon sticks
- 1 tablespoon fish sauce
- 1 tablespoon sugar

Instructions:

1. In a pot, sauté the Massaman curry paste until fragrant.
2. Add coconut milk, chicken broth, chicken, and potatoes. Simmer for 30 minutes.
3. Add peanuts, cinnamon sticks, fish sauce, and sugar.
4. Simmer for an additional 15 minutes and serve with rice.

Khao Pad (Thai Fried Rice)

Ingredients:

- 2 cups cooked jasmine rice (preferably cold)
- 1/2 lb shrimp or chicken, sliced
- 2 eggs, beaten
- 1/2 onion, chopped
- 2 cloves garlic, minced
- 2 tablespoons fish sauce
- 1 tablespoon soy sauce
- 1 tablespoon oyster sauce
- 1/4 cup green onions, chopped
- Lime wedges for garnish

Instructions:

1. In a wok, heat oil and sauté garlic and onion.
2. Add shrimp or chicken and cook until browned.
3. Push to the side, add beaten eggs, and scramble them.
4. Add rice, fish sauce, soy sauce, and oyster sauce. Stir-fry until well combined.
5. Garnish with green onions and lime wedges, and serve hot.

Goong Pad Saparot (Pineapple Fried Rice with Shrimp)

Ingredients:

- 1/2 lb shrimp, peeled and deveined
- 2 cups cold jasmine rice
- 1 small pineapple, peeled and chopped
- 2 eggs, beaten
- 1/4 cup cashews
- 1/4 cup raisins
- 2 tablespoons soy sauce
- 1 tablespoon fish sauce
- 1 tablespoon curry powder
- Green onions for garnish

Instructions:

1. In a wok, heat oil and cook shrimp until pink. Remove and set aside.
2. In the same wok, scramble the eggs, then add rice, pineapple, cashews, and raisins.
3. Season with soy sauce, fish sauce, and curry powder. Stir-fry to combine.
4. Add cooked shrimp and toss to mix. Garnish with green onions.

Nam Tok Moo (Grilled Pork Salad)

Ingredients:

- 1 lb pork shoulder or pork belly
- 2 tablespoons fish sauce
- 2 tablespoons lime juice
- 1 tablespoon chili flakes
- 1 tablespoon roasted rice powder
- 1/2 red onion, thinly sliced
- Fresh cilantro for garnish

Instructions:

1. Grill the pork until cooked through, then slice thinly.
2. In a bowl, mix fish sauce, lime juice, chili flakes, and roasted rice powder.
3. Add the pork, red onion, and cilantro, and toss to coat.
4. Serve immediately with rice.

Khao Niew Mamuang (Mango Sticky Rice)

Ingredients:

- 1 cup sticky rice
- 1 1/2 cups coconut milk
- 1/2 cup sugar
- 1/4 teaspoon salt
- 2 ripe mangoes, peeled and sliced
- Sesame seeds for garnish (optional)

Instructions:

1. Cook sticky rice according to package instructions.
2. In a saucepan, heat coconut milk, sugar, and salt until the sugar dissolves.
3. Pour coconut milk mixture over cooked sticky rice and stir to combine.
4. Serve the sticky rice with mango slices and garnish with sesame seeds.

Tom Yum Goong Nam Khon (Creamy Spicy Shrimp Soup)

Ingredients:

- 1 lb shrimp, peeled and deveined
- 4 cups chicken broth
- 3 stalks lemongrass, smashed
- 5-6 kaffir lime leaves, torn
- 3-4 Thai bird's eye chilies, smashed
- 2-3 cloves garlic, minced
- 1/2 cup coconut milk
- 2 tablespoons fish sauce
- 1 tablespoon lime juice
- Fresh cilantro for garnish
- Thai chili paste (optional)

Instructions:

1. Bring chicken broth to a boil, adding lemongrass, lime leaves, chilies, and garlic.
2. Simmer for 10 minutes to infuse the flavors.
3. Add shrimp and cook for 3-4 minutes, then stir in coconut milk, fish sauce, and lime juice.
4. Adjust seasoning with extra lime juice or fish sauce if needed.
5. Garnish with fresh cilantro and serve hot.

Hor Mok (Steamed Fish Curry)

Ingredients:

- 1 lb white fish fillets (such as tilapia or snapper)
- 1/4 cup red curry paste
- 1/2 cup coconut milk
- 1 egg
- 2 tablespoons fish sauce
- 1 tablespoon palm sugar
- 2 kaffir lime leaves, finely shredded
- Fresh basil or cilantro for garnish
- Banana leaves or ramekins for steaming

Instructions:

1. Blend the fish fillets with curry paste, coconut milk, egg, fish sauce, and palm sugar until smooth.
2. Spoon the mixture into banana leaves or small ramekins.
3. Steam over simmering water for 15-20 minutes until firm and cooked through.
4. Garnish with kaffir lime leaves and fresh basil or cilantro before serving.

Moo Satay (Grilled Pork Skewers)

Ingredients:

- 1 lb pork tenderloin, cut into strips
- 2 tablespoons curry powder
- 1 tablespoon turmeric powder
- 2 tablespoons soy sauce
- 1 tablespoon fish sauce
- 1 tablespoon sugar
- 1 tablespoon coconut milk
- 1 tablespoon vegetable oil
- Bamboo skewers (soaked in water)
- Peanut sauce for serving

Instructions:

1. In a bowl, mix curry powder, turmeric, soy sauce, fish sauce, sugar, coconut milk, and oil to form the marinade.
2. Thread pork strips onto soaked bamboo skewers and marinate for at least 1 hour.
3. Grill the skewers over medium heat for 4-5 minutes on each side until golden and cooked through.
4. Serve with peanut sauce.

Kanom Jeen (Rice Noodles with Curry)

Ingredients:

- 1 lb rice noodles
- 1/2 lb chicken or beef, thinly sliced
- 2 tablespoons curry paste (yellow or green)
- 1 cup coconut milk
- 1 tablespoon fish sauce
- 1 tablespoon palm sugar
- 1 cup bean sprouts
- Fresh cilantro and mint for garnish

Instructions:

1. Cook rice noodles according to package instructions and set aside.
2. In a pan, heat curry paste and cook for 1-2 minutes until fragrant.
3. Add coconut milk, fish sauce, and palm sugar. Bring to a simmer, then add meat and cook until done.
4. Serve noodles topped with the curry sauce, bean sprouts, and fresh herbs.

Baked Mussels with Glass Noodles

Ingredients:

- 12-16 fresh mussels, cleaned
- 1/2 cup glass noodles (soaked in warm water)
- 2 tablespoons garlic, minced
- 2 tablespoons fish sauce
- 1 tablespoon soy sauce
- 1 tablespoon sugar
- 1/4 cup cilantro, chopped
- 2 tablespoons lime juice

Instructions:

1. Preheat oven to 375°F (190°C).
2. Mix the soaked glass noodles with garlic, fish sauce, soy sauce, sugar, and lime juice.
3. Place mussels on a baking sheet, top each with the noodle mixture.
4. Bake for 10-15 minutes until mussels open and noodles are tender.
5. Garnish with fresh cilantro and serve.

Gaeng Kari (Yellow Curry)

Ingredients:

- 1 lb chicken, beef, or tofu, cubed
- 2 tablespoons yellow curry paste
- 1 can coconut milk
- 1 cup chicken broth
- 2 potatoes, cubed
- 1 onion, chopped
- 1 tablespoon fish sauce
- 1 tablespoon palm sugar
- Fresh cilantro for garnish

Instructions:

1. In a pot, sauté curry paste until fragrant, then add coconut milk and chicken broth.
2. Add chicken or tofu and potatoes. Simmer for 20 minutes until tender.
3. Season with fish sauce and sugar, adjusting to taste.
4. Serve with rice and garnish with cilantro.

Pad Krapow Gai (Basil Chicken Stir-Fry)

Ingredients:

- 1 lb ground chicken
- 2 tablespoons vegetable oil
- 3 cloves garlic, minced
- 2-3 bird's eye chilies, chopped
- 2 tablespoons fish sauce
- 1 tablespoon soy sauce
- 1 tablespoon oyster sauce
- 1 tablespoon sugar
- 1 cup Thai basil leaves
- Steamed rice for serving

Instructions:

1. Heat oil in a wok and sauté garlic and chilies until fragrant.
2. Add ground chicken and cook until browned.
3. Stir in fish sauce, soy sauce, oyster sauce, and sugar. Cook for 2-3 minutes.
4. Add basil leaves and stir-fry until wilted.
5. Serve over steamed rice.

Kaeng Phet (Spicy Red Curry)

Ingredients:

- 1 lb chicken, beef, or tofu, cubed
- 2 tablespoons red curry paste
- 1 can coconut milk
- 1 cup chicken broth
- 1 red bell pepper, sliced
- 1 zucchini, sliced
- 1 tablespoon fish sauce
- 1 tablespoon sugar
- Fresh basil for garnish

Instructions:

1. Heat curry paste in a pot until fragrant, then add coconut milk and chicken broth.
2. Add meat or tofu and vegetables. Simmer for 15-20 minutes until cooked.
3. Season with fish sauce and sugar, adjusting to taste.
4. Serve with rice and garnish with fresh basil.

Khai Jiao (Thai Omelette)

Ingredients:

- 3 eggs
- 2 tablespoons fish sauce
- 1 tablespoon soy sauce
- 1 tablespoon vegetable oil
- Fresh cilantro for garnish

Instructions:

1. Beat eggs with fish sauce and soy sauce.
2. Heat oil in a frying pan over medium heat, then pour in the egg mixture.
3. Cook until golden on both sides, flipping carefully.
4. Garnish with fresh cilantro and serve with rice.

Tod Man Pla (Thai Fish Cakes)

Ingredients:

- 1 lb white fish fillets, minced
- 2 tablespoons red curry paste
- 1 tablespoon fish sauce
- 1 tablespoon lime juice
- 1 egg
- 1/4 cup green beans, chopped
- 1/4 cup cilantro, chopped
- 1/2 cup breadcrumbs
- Vegetable oil for frying

Instructions:

1. Mix fish, curry paste, fish sauce, lime juice, egg, green beans, cilantro, and breadcrumbs until well combined.
2. Shape the mixture into small patties.
3. Heat oil in a pan and fry the patties until golden and crispy.
4. Serve with sweet chili sauce.

Yum Nua (Spicy Beef Salad)

Ingredients:

- 1 lb beef (sirloin or flank steak), grilled and sliced thinly
- 1 cucumber, sliced
- 1/2 red onion, thinly sliced
- 1 cup cherry tomatoes, halved
- 1/4 cup cilantro, chopped
- 2-3 bird's eye chilies, chopped (optional)
- 2 tablespoons fish sauce
- 1 tablespoon lime juice
- 1 tablespoon sugar
- 1 tablespoon toasted rice powder (optional)
- Fresh mint leaves for garnish

Instructions:

1. Grill the beef and slice it thinly against the grain.
2. In a bowl, combine the beef with cucumber, red onion, cherry tomatoes, and cilantro.
3. Mix the fish sauce, lime juice, sugar, and chilies in a separate bowl, then pour it over the beef mixture.
4. Sprinkle with toasted rice powder, if using.
5. Garnish with fresh mint leaves and serve.

Tom Zap (Sour and Spicy Soup)

Ingredients:

- 1 lb pork or beef, thinly sliced
- 4 cups chicken broth
- 2 stalks lemongrass, smashed
- 5-6 kaffir lime leaves, torn
- 3-4 bird's eye chilies, smashed
- 3-4 cloves garlic, minced
- 2 tablespoons fish sauce
- 1 tablespoon lime juice
- 1-2 tomatoes, chopped
- Fresh cilantro for garnish

Instructions:

1. Bring the chicken broth to a boil and add the lemongrass, lime leaves, chilies, and garlic. Let it simmer for 10 minutes to infuse the flavors.
2. Add the meat and cook until tender.
3. Add the tomatoes and continue cooking for another 5 minutes.
4. Season with fish sauce and lime juice, adjusting to taste.
5. Garnish with fresh cilantro and serve hot.

Khao Mun Gai (Chicken Rice)

Ingredients:

- 1 whole chicken
- 2 cups jasmine rice
- 1 tablespoon vegetable oil
- 1 cucumber, sliced
- Fresh cilantro for garnish

For the sauce:

- 3 tablespoons soy sauce
- 1 tablespoon sugar
- 1 tablespoon lime juice
- 2-3 cloves garlic, minced
- 1 tablespoon chili paste (optional)

Instructions:

1. Boil the chicken in a pot of water for 40 minutes, reserving the broth. Remove the chicken and set aside.
2. Rinse the rice, then cook it in a pot with 1 tablespoon of vegetable oil and 1.5 cups of the chicken broth.
3. For the sauce, mix soy sauce, sugar, lime juice, garlic, and chili paste (if using) in a small saucepan. Heat until the sugar dissolves.
4. Serve the rice with sliced chicken, cucumber, and a drizzle of the sauce, garnished with cilantro.

Kuay Tiew (Thai Noodle Soup)

Ingredients:

- 1 lb pork or chicken, thinly sliced
- 4 cups chicken broth
- 1 tablespoon soy sauce
- 1 tablespoon fish sauce
- 2-3 cloves garlic, minced
- 1 cup rice noodles
- 2-3 baby bok choy, chopped
- Fresh cilantro for garnish
- Lime wedges for serving

Instructions:

1. Bring the chicken broth to a boil, then add garlic, soy sauce, and fish sauce. Simmer for 10 minutes.
2. Add the pork or chicken and cook until tender.
3. Cook the rice noodles according to package instructions.
4. To serve, place noodles in a bowl, top with soup and meat, and add bok choy.
5. Garnish with fresh cilantro and serve with lime wedges.

Pla Rad Prik (Fried Fish with Chili Sauce)

Ingredients:

- 1 whole fish (tilapia or snapper), cleaned and gutted
- 1/4 cup all-purpose flour
- 2 tablespoons vegetable oil for frying
- 1/4 cup fish sauce
- 1 tablespoon sugar
- 2-3 tablespoons lime juice
- 3-4 bird's eye chilies, chopped
- 2 cloves garlic, minced
- Fresh cilantro for garnish

Instructions:

1. Coat the fish in flour and fry it in hot oil until crispy and golden, about 6-8 minutes per side.
2. In a separate pan, heat the fish sauce, sugar, lime juice, chilies, and garlic. Simmer for 3-4 minutes until the sauce thickens slightly.
3. Pour the sauce over the fried fish and garnish with fresh cilantro.
4. Serve with steamed rice.

Moo Hong (Braised Pork Belly)

Ingredients:

- 1 lb pork belly, cut into chunks
- 2 tablespoons vegetable oil
- 3-4 cloves garlic, minced
- 1 tablespoon soy sauce
- 1 tablespoon fish sauce
- 1 tablespoon sugar
- 1 cup water
- 2-3 star anise
- 2-3 cinnamon sticks
- Fresh cilantro for garnish

Instructions:

1. Heat oil in a pot and sauté the garlic until fragrant.
2. Add the pork belly and brown it on all sides.
3. Add soy sauce, fish sauce, sugar, water, star anise, and cinnamon sticks.
4. Simmer for 45 minutes to 1 hour until the pork is tender and the sauce thickens.
5. Garnish with cilantro and serve with steamed rice.

Gaeng Pa (Jungle Curry)

Ingredients:

- 1 lb chicken or pork, sliced
- 2 tablespoons red curry paste
- 1 can coconut milk
- 2 cups chicken broth
- 1 eggplant, chopped
- 1 bell pepper, chopped
- 1 zucchini, sliced
- 2-3 kaffir lime leaves
- Fresh basil for garnish

Instructions:

1. Heat curry paste in a pot until fragrant, then add coconut milk and chicken broth.
2. Add the chicken or pork and vegetables. Simmer for 20 minutes until the vegetables are tender.
3. Add kaffir lime leaves and basil, cooking for another 5 minutes.
4. Serve with rice and garnish with fresh basil.

Kanom Krok (Coconut Rice Pancakes)

Ingredients:

- 1 cup rice flour
- 1/2 cup coconut milk
- 1/4 cup sugar
- 1/4 teaspoon salt
- 1/2 cup shredded coconut
- 2 tablespoons vegetable oil for greasing

Instructions:

1. Mix rice flour, coconut milk, sugar, and salt in a bowl to form a smooth batter.
2. Preheat a kanom krok pan or non-stick skillet, and lightly grease with vegetable oil.
3. Pour the batter into the pan, filling each mold about halfway.
4. Sprinkle shredded coconut on top and cook until golden brown on both sides, about 2-3 minutes.
5. Serve warm.

Yod Woon Sen (Glass Noodle Salad)

Ingredients:

- 1 lb ground pork or chicken
- 1 package glass noodles
- 1 cucumber, sliced
- 1/2 cup cherry tomatoes, halved
- 1/4 cup cilantro, chopped
- 2-3 tablespoons fish sauce
- 1 tablespoon lime juice
- 1 tablespoon sugar
- 2-3 bird's eye chilies, chopped

Instructions:

1. Cook glass noodles according to package instructions, then drain and set aside.
2. Cook the ground meat in a pan until browned and cooked through.
3. In a bowl, combine noodles, meat, cucumber, tomatoes, and cilantro.
4. In a separate bowl, mix fish sauce, lime juice, sugar, and chilies, then pour over the noodle mixture.
5. Toss everything together and serve.

Moo Pad King (Stir-Fried Pork with Ginger)

Ingredients:

- 1 lb pork (tenderloin or shoulder), thinly sliced
- 1/4 cup ginger, julienned
- 2-3 cloves garlic, minced
- 2 tablespoons soy sauce
- 1 tablespoon fish sauce
- 1 tablespoon sugar
- 1 tablespoon vegetable oil
- 1/4 cup bell pepper, sliced
- Fresh cilantro for garnish

Instructions:

1. Heat oil in a wok and sauté garlic and ginger until fragrant.
2. Add the sliced pork and cook until browned.
3. Add soy sauce, fish sauce, and sugar, stirring to coat the pork.
4. Add bell pepper and cook for another 2-3 minutes until tender.
5. Garnish with cilantro and serve with rice.

Moo Nam Tok (Waterfall Pork Salad)

Ingredients:

- 1 lb pork shoulder or pork belly, grilled and thinly sliced
- 1/2 red onion, thinly sliced
- 1/2 cucumber, sliced
- 1/4 cup cilantro, chopped
- 2-3 bird's eye chilies, chopped
- 2 tablespoons fish sauce
- 1 tablespoon lime juice
- 1 tablespoon toasted rice powder (optional)
- 1 tablespoon sugar
- Fresh mint leaves for garnish

Instructions:

1. Grill the pork until charred and cooked through, then slice thinly.
2. In a bowl, combine the grilled pork with onion, cucumber, cilantro, and chilies.
3. In a separate bowl, mix fish sauce, lime juice, toasted rice powder, and sugar to create a dressing.
4. Pour the dressing over the salad and toss well.
5. Garnish with mint leaves and serve.

Goong Mung Krob (Crispy Shrimp)

Ingredients:

- 1 lb large shrimp, peeled and deveined
- 1/4 cup rice flour
- 1/4 cup cornstarch
- 1/2 teaspoon baking powder
- 1/2 teaspoon salt
- 1/4 teaspoon white pepper
- 1 cup cold water
- Vegetable oil for frying
- Sweet chili sauce for dipping

Instructions:

1. In a bowl, mix rice flour, cornstarch, baking powder, salt, and pepper. Add cold water to make a smooth batter.
2. Heat oil in a deep pan or wok to 350°F (175°C).
3. Dip shrimp into the batter and fry them in batches until golden and crispy, about 3-4 minutes.
4. Drain on paper towels and serve with sweet chili sauce.

Khao Pad Kung (Shrimp Fried Rice)

Ingredients:

- 2 cups cooked jasmine rice (preferably day-old)
- 1 lb shrimp, peeled and deveined
- 2 eggs, beaten
- 1/2 onion, chopped
- 2-3 cloves garlic, minced
- 2 tablespoons fish sauce
- 1 tablespoon soy sauce
- 1 tablespoon oyster sauce
- 1/4 cup peas and carrots (optional)
- 1/4 cup green onions, chopped
- 1/4 cup cilantro, chopped
- Lime wedges for garnish

Instructions:

1. In a wok or large pan, heat oil and sauté garlic and onion until fragrant.
2. Add shrimp and cook until pink, then remove from the pan.
3. Add the beaten eggs to the pan, scramble, and cook through.
4. Add the rice, fish sauce, soy sauce, and oyster sauce. Stir well to combine.
5. Add shrimp, peas, carrots, green onions, and cilantro. Stir until evenly mixed.
6. Serve with lime wedges.

Pad Kee Mao (Drunken Noodles)

Ingredients:

- 1 lb rice noodles
- 1/2 lb chicken, beef, or pork, thinly sliced
- 2-3 cloves garlic, minced
- 2-3 bird's eye chilies, chopped
- 1/2 cup Thai basil leaves
- 1/4 cup bell peppers, sliced
- 2 tablespoons fish sauce
- 1 tablespoon soy sauce
- 1 tablespoon oyster sauce
- 1 tablespoon sugar
- 1/4 cup chicken broth or water
- Vegetable oil for stir-frying

Instructions:

1. Cook rice noodles according to package instructions, then drain.
2. In a wok, heat oil and sauté garlic and chilies until fragrant.
3. Add meat and cook until browned.
4. Add bell peppers, fish sauce, soy sauce, oyster sauce, and sugar. Stir to combine.
5. Add noodles and chicken broth, stir-frying until everything is well mixed.
6. Add basil leaves and stir until wilted. Serve hot.

Som Tum Thai (Spicy Thai Papaya Salad)

Ingredients:

- 1 green papaya, peeled and shredded
- 2-3 cloves garlic
- 2-3 bird's eye chilies
- 1/4 cup fish sauce
- 1/4 cup lime juice
- 2 tablespoons sugar
- 1/4 cup cherry tomatoes, halved
- 1/4 cup green beans, cut into 2-inch pieces
- 1/4 cup roasted peanuts, crushed
- 1/4 cup dried shrimp (optional)

Instructions:

1. In a mortar and pestle, pound garlic, chilies, fish sauce, lime juice, and sugar to create a dressing.
2. In a large bowl, mix shredded papaya, tomatoes, green beans, peanuts, and dried shrimp.
3. Pour the dressing over the papaya mixture and toss to combine.
4. Serve immediately with sticky rice.

Gai Pad Med Mamuang (Chicken with Cashew Nuts)

Ingredients:

- 1 lb chicken breast, thinly sliced
- 1/2 cup roasted cashew nuts
- 2 tablespoons vegetable oil
- 1/4 cup bell peppers, sliced
- 1/4 cup onion, sliced
- 1/4 cup carrots, sliced
- 2-3 cloves garlic, minced
- 2 tablespoons soy sauce
- 1 tablespoon oyster sauce
- 1 tablespoon sugar
- 1 tablespoon fish sauce
- 1/4 cup water or chicken broth

Instructions:

1. Heat oil in a pan or wok and sauté garlic until fragrant.
2. Add chicken and cook until browned.
3. Add vegetables, soy sauce, oyster sauce, sugar, fish sauce, and water. Stir-fry for 3-4 minutes.
4. Add cashew nuts and stir to combine.
5. Serve with rice.

Nam Prik Ong (Spicy Tomato Dip)

Ingredients:

- 2-3 medium tomatoes, roasted or boiled
- 1/2 lb ground pork
- 2-3 cloves garlic
- 2-3 bird's eye chilies
- 2 tablespoons fish sauce
- 1 tablespoon soy sauce
- 1 tablespoon lime juice
- Fresh cilantro for garnish

Instructions:

1. Roast or boil tomatoes until soft, then blend or mash them.
2. In a pan, cook the ground pork until browned, then set aside.
3. In a mortar, pound garlic and chilies until fine, then add tomatoes and pound together.
4. Add fish sauce, soy sauce, lime juice, and cooked pork to the mixture. Stir to combine.
5. Garnish with cilantro and serve with fresh vegetables or rice.

Pad Pak Bung Fai Daeng (Stir-Fried Morning Glory)

Ingredients:

- 1 lb morning glory (water spinach), washed and chopped
- 2 tablespoons vegetable oil
- 2-3 cloves garlic, minced
- 2-3 bird's eye chilies, chopped
- 1 tablespoon fish sauce
- 1 tablespoon soy sauce
- 1 tablespoon oyster sauce
- 1 tablespoon sugar

Instructions:

1. Heat oil in a wok and sauté garlic and chilies until fragrant.
2. Add morning glory and stir-fry for 2-3 minutes until wilted.
3. Add fish sauce, soy sauce, oyster sauce, and sugar. Stir to combine.
4. Serve hot with rice.

Pla Nueng Manao (Steamed Fish with Lime)

Ingredients:

- 1 whole fish (tilapia or snapper), cleaned and gutted
- 3-4 cloves garlic, minced
- 2-3 bird's eye chilies, chopped
- 1/4 cup fish sauce
- 1/4 cup lime juice
- 1 tablespoon sugar
- Fresh cilantro for garnish

Instructions:

1. Steam the fish for 15-20 minutes until fully cooked.
2. In a small bowl, mix garlic, chilies, fish sauce, lime juice, and sugar to create the sauce.
3. Pour the sauce over the steamed fish and garnish with cilantro.
4. Serve with rice.

Khao Chae (Rice in Jasmine Scented Water)

Ingredients:

- 2 cups jasmine rice
- 4 cups water
- 1/4 cup coconut milk
- 1 tablespoon sugar
- 2-3 pandan leaves (optional)

Instructions:

1. Rinse the rice until the water runs clear, then cook it in water with pandan leaves for fragrance.
2. In a separate pot, bring coconut milk and sugar to a boil. Remove from heat and set aside.
3. Serve the rice in small bowls with jasmine-scented water and drizzle with coconut milk.

Nua Pad Prik (Beef with Chili Sauce)

Ingredients:

- 1 lb beef, thinly sliced
- 2-3 cloves garlic, minced
- 2-3 bird's eye chilies, chopped
- 2 tablespoons soy sauce
- 1 tablespoon oyster sauce
- 1 tablespoon fish sauce
- 1 tablespoon sugar
- Fresh cilantro for garnish

Instructions:

1. In a pan or wok, heat oil and sauté garlic and chilies until fragrant.
2. Add beef and cook until browned.
3. Add soy sauce, oyster sauce, fish sauce, and sugar. Stir to combine.
4. Garnish with cilantro and serve with rice.